Native Americans of the Plains

by Deborah Kops

Table of Contents

Pictures To Think About i
Words To Think About iii
Introduction 2
CHAPTER 1 Traditional Ways of Life 4
CHAPTER 2 Conflicts and Struggles 14
CHAPTER 3 Modern Life 22
Conclusion 29
Glossary 31
Index 32

Pictures To Think About

Native Americans of the Plains

Words To Think About

Characteristics
- area of land
- owned by tribes
- ?

Examples
- Pine Ridge, South Dakota
- Alabama-Coushatta, Texas
- ?

reservation
What do you think the word **reservation** means?

tan
What do you think the word **tan** means in this book?

Meaning 1
a light brown color (noun)

Meaning 2
to lie in the sun (verb)

Meaning 3
to make animal skin into leather (verb)

iii

Read for More Clues

conflict, page 14
reservation, page 3
tan, page 17

conflict

What do you think the word **conflict** means?

What starts a **conflict**?
- fighting over land
- ?
- cruelty

How can you end a **conflict**?
- winning the war
- ?
- talking

iv

Introduction

Before the 1800s, most **Plains** Indians lived on the Great Plains. Plains are flat, grassy lands. The Great Plains are east of the Rocky Mountains. They are west of the Mississippi River. Many buffalo once roamed these lands.

By the 1700s, this region had more than thirty tribes. A tribe is a group of people that live together. Tribes share ways of life. At first, the Plains tribes lived in villages. Later, they became **nomads** (NOH-madz). They traveled from place to place. They followed the buffalo. Tribes hunted buffalo for food and clothes.

▲ Native Americans have lived on the Great Plains for at least 15,000 years.

In time, life on the Plains changed. White people settled on the Great Plains. They took land. White hunters killed almost all of the buffalo.

In this book, you will learn about the Plains Indians. You will see how they lived in the past. You will see how they live on **reservations** (reh-zer-VAY-shunz) today. You will see how these people had to **adapt** (uh-DAPT), or change. You will see how they lived in hard times. You will also see how they keep their customs alive today.

Read on to meet the great people of the Great Plains!

▲ The Great Plains extend from Texas to Canada. This map shows where the main Plains Indian tribes lived.

CHAPTER 1

Traditional
Ways of Life

Before the 1700s, most Plains Indians lived in villages. Tribes lived near rivers. They fished and grew food. A few men hunted buffalo. Hunting was difficult. The Plains Indians did not have horses. They had to walk long distances to find the buffalo. The hunters and their families slept in **tepees** (TEE-peez). Tepees are like tents. When tribes moved, they used dogs to pull their things.

▲ Preparing a buffalo hide was a woman's job. A woman sometimes spent ten days getting one hide ready to use.

In the early 1700s, southwest Indian tribes brought horses to the Plains. The Plains people had never seen horses before. They called them mystery dogs. The Plains people learned to ride. Hunters followed the herds. They could hunt more easily.

With horses, many Plains tribes began to hunt all year. These tribes stopped living in villages. Instead, they became nomads.

The Plains Indians used almost every part of a buffalo. Women used the meat to make stews. They made the skins into tepees and clothes. They made bones into tools and sleds. The buffalo gave the people almost all they needed.

IT'S A FACT

The Plains Indians did not all speak the same language. So, they developed a sign language. They spoke to each other with their hands.

▲ The Plains Indians moved camp often. They loaded their goods onto a travois (truh-VOY), a frame slung between poles and pulled by a dog or horse.

CHAPTER 1

The Comanche

The Comanche (kuh-MAN-chee) were one tribe. This tribe lived on the southern plains. They became great horseback riders. They were also good hunters. Boys and girls began riding at a very young age. Most boys had their own horse at five.

Comanche men hunted in groups called bands. Most of the other tribes hunted in bands, too.

Over time, bands formed larger groups called divisions. These divisions were named for favorite Comanche foods. One was called the Root Eaters. The Buffalo Eaters was the name of another group. Can you guess what the Honey Eaters liked to eat?

▲ 1844 engraving of a Comanche village

TRADITIONAL WAYS OF LIFE

In time, the Comanche had many horses. Wild horses roamed their lands. The Comanche learned to capture the wild horses. The Comanche waited where the horses went to drink. Then they used ropes to catch the horses.

Horses were very valuable. They were symbols of wealth. The Comanche became a rich tribe. They had thousands of horses. They claimed much land for hunting.

MATH MATTERS

In 1700, there were about 7,000 Comanche people. By 1750, there were about 20,000 Comanche. As the Comanche grew wealthier, their population grew.

▼ The Comanche depended on their horses. They honored them and took good care of them.

CHAPTER 1

The Plains Villages

The Comanche were nomads. Other tribes, like the Hidatsa (HEE-daht-sah), stayed in one place. This tribe lived in villages. The villages were near rivers on the northern plains. The seasons controlled their lives.

In spring, they planted crops. They planted corn, beans, and green vegetables. When the plants were strong, most people left the village. They went to the grasslands to hunt buffalo. In the summer, they returned home to pick their crops. After the harvest, they went on one last hunt. They needed meat for the winter.

▼ After the harvest, tribes often held celebrations.

IT'S A FACT

Every tribe preserved buffalo meat for the winter. The women roasted some of the meat and pounded it into a paste. It was called pemmican. They also dried some meat in the sun.

TRADITIONAL WAYS OF LIFE

The Hidatsa women were good gardeners. They grew five types of beans in their gardens. They grew nine types of corn. They also grew squash. The women dried some vegetables in the sun. Then they stored the vegetables away for the winter.

Women often grew more food than their families could eat. Other tribes came to the villages to trade. Other tribes traded buffalo skins and meat for corn and beans. Soon, the villages became trading centers.

▼ Most people in villages lived in lodges. An earth-covered lodge lasted about ten years.

CHAPTER 1

Family and Society

The Plains Indians had strong family ties. Mothers and fathers cared for their children. So did other family members. A grandfather might take a boy on his first hunting trip. An aunt might teach a girl how to prepare a buffalo skin.

✓ POINT

Reread

Reread the information about family life as a Plains Indian. If you could go back in time to visit, what might you learn from the children your age? What might you teach them?

Brothers and sisters played together. They also helped the adults. They set up tepees. Boys pretended to hunt buffalo. Girls sewed robes. Games and chores prepared children for the future.

▲ These are Sioux chiefs.

TRADITIONAL WAYS OF LIFE

Cousins teased one another. Teasing was sometimes a way of teaching a lesson. It taught someone not to break the rules of the tribe.

It was important to follow the rules. Winters could be hard on the Great Plains. People needed one another. Sometimes a man went hunting alone, without his band. The man was punished for being selfish. The tribe's police might destroy his home as a lesson.

Police kept peace and order in the hunting band. Chiefs kept peace within the tribe and with other tribes. Each tribe had several chiefs. The Cheyenne (shy-AN) tribe had forty-four chiefs!

HISTORICAL PERSPECTIVE

The Plains Indians joined all sorts of societies, which were like clubs. Most were for either men or women, but not both. In the Arapaho (uh-RA-puh-hoh) tribe, some women joined a society for quillworkers. They attached porcupine quills to clothing, cradles, and other things as decoration. Many tribes had warrior societies for men who fought in wars. The Tall Ones was a society for brave Sioux (SOO) warriors. Each member promised that he would put his own life at risk to save another Sioux warrior. Today, many members of tribes still belong to different societies.

CHAPTER 1

Customs and Ceremonies

Every summer, the hunting bands from a tribe came together. They met at a campsite. They brought their horses and dogs. They set up their tepees in a big circle. At sunset, their campfires lit up the sky.

IT'S A FACT

The Plains people valued generosity. The Sioux held a ceremony that called for great generosity. A father held a ball-throwing ceremony when his daughter became a teenager. She threw a red ball into a crowd of guests. Each time someone caught the ball, he or she received a wonderful gift, such as a horse.

▲ Part of the Sun Dance ceremony took place in a special lodge. It looked like a giant tepee without a cover.

TRADITIONAL WAYS OF LIFE

The tribe did many things together. The men went hunting. Young people raced their horses. Everyone took part in special traditions.

Many tribes held a Sun Dance at their gatherings. The Plains Indians wanted to get closer to nature. They sang, danced, and beat their drums for days.

THE VISION QUEST

One of the most important ceremonies for the Plains Indians was the vision quest. All of the tribes believed that mysterious forces affected a person's life. It was important to get in touch with these forces. So a member, usually a boy or man, went to a quiet place. He stayed for four days without any food or drink. He hoped to have a dream or vision. The dream might be about an animal or an insect. Each one had a different meaning. The Crow tribe believed that if someone dreamed of a mosquito, he would become one of the leaders of his tribe.

The Plains Indians wanted to feel pure and clean before taking part in an important ceremony. So they sat in a sweat lodge. They heated some rocks. When the rocks were very hot, they poured water on them. That made steam rise. Sitting in the hot, steamy lodge, the Indians felt refreshed.

CHAPTER 2

Conflicts
and Struggles

In the 1840s, many white settlers crossed the Great Plains. The settlers were on their way west. Some wanted to start farms. Others wanted to find gold.

At first, the tribes and the settlers got along. Then things changed. Some settlers killed buffalo. The wagons disturbed the herds. The herds changed their habits. They stayed away from the hunting lands. This hurt the tribes. Soon, fighting began. Years of **conflict** (KAHN-flikt) followed.

MATH MATTERS

In 1849, during one six-week period, 40,000 people came through the Great Plains on their way to California and Oregon. That is more than 6,000 people per week.

The United States government wanted settlers to be able to travel safely. In 1851, leaders met with the Plains tribes. Ten thousand Plains people came.

The leaders asked each tribe to stay on its hunting lands. The Plains people agreed. Peace lasted a few years. Then the fighting started again.

IT'S A FACT

The families who crossed the Great Plains sometimes left deadly germs behind. In 1849, there was a cholera (KAH-luh-ruh) epidemic in the Kiowa (KY-uh-wah) and Comanche tribes. An epidemic does not spread slowly. It races through a population. Many Comanche and Kiowa died. When white people and Native Americans first came in contact with each other, Native Americans often became sick. Their bodies did not have a chance to build up resistance to the new germs.

▲ Pioneers traveled across the plains in covered wagons.

CHAPTER 2

The Buffalo Disappear

In the 1860s, the buffalo began to disappear. White hunters from the East went to the Plains. Buffalo hides were a big business. Hunters could make a lot of money. The more hides a hunter sent back, the richer he became.

Two causes made buffalo hides valuable. One was the railroads. Trains were fast and cheap. Trains were an easy way to get the hides back east. Hunters could make more money for each hide.

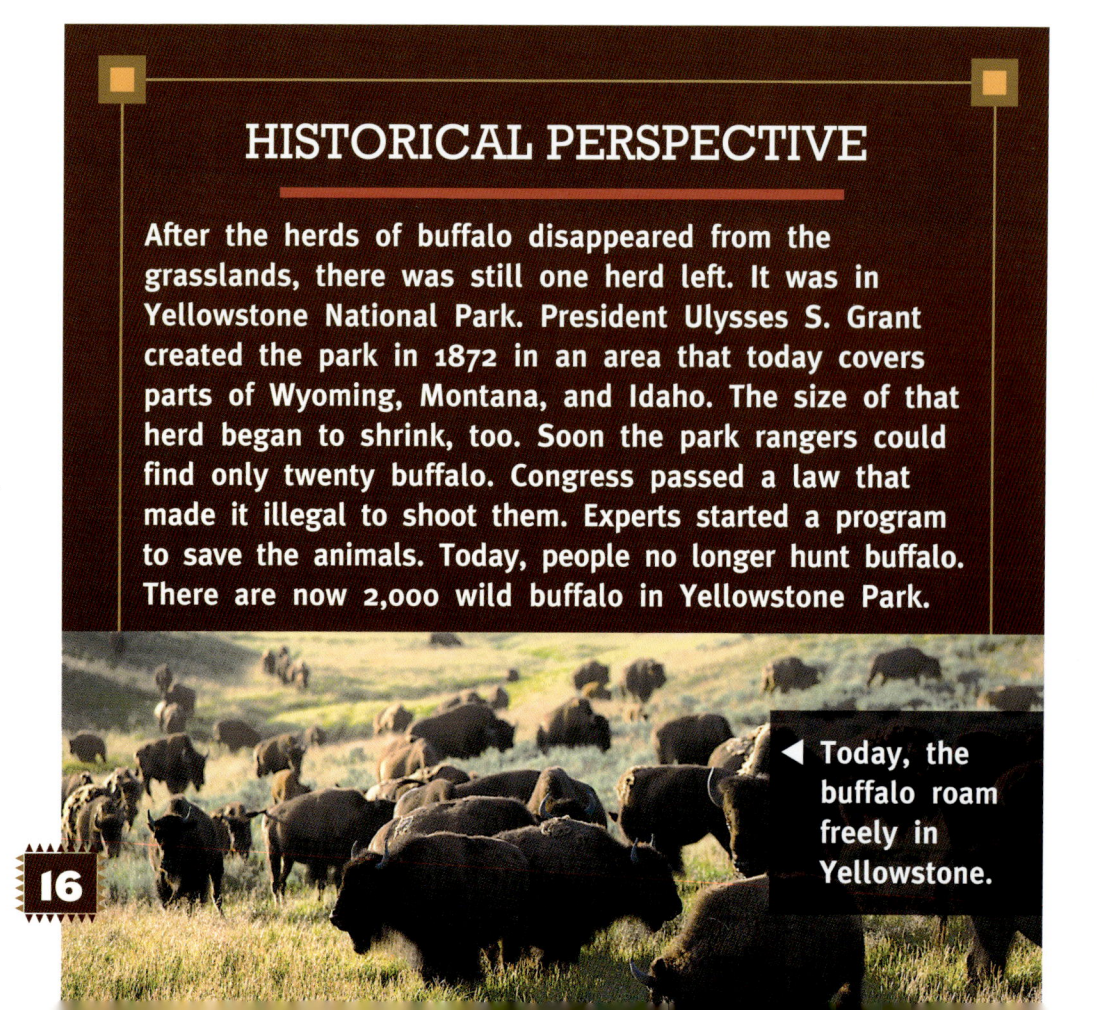

HISTORICAL PERSPECTIVE

After the herds of buffalo disappeared from the grasslands, there was still one herd left. It was in Yellowstone National Park. President Ulysses S. Grant created the park in 1872 in an area that today covers parts of Wyoming, Montana, and Idaho. The size of that herd began to shrink, too. Soon the park rangers could find only twenty buffalo. Congress passed a law that made it illegal to shoot them. Experts started a program to save the animals. Today, people no longer hunt buffalo. There are now 2,000 wild buffalo in Yellowstone Park.

◀ Today, the buffalo roam freely in Yellowstone.

CONFLICTS AND STRUGGLES

The other cause was demand. **Tanned** buffalo skins were popular. Tanners were people who tanned buffalo skins. Tanners made the tough skins into leather. In 1870, tanners learned how to make the skins into a softer leather. They used the soft leather to make shoes, wallets, and belts. Many people wanted these soft leather goods. This demand made the hides very valuable.

White hunters killed millions of buffalo each year. By 1880, the herds were almost gone. In 1884, the last load of skins left the Great Plains.

The buffalo were gone. The Plains Indians' way of life disappeared, too.

▲ James Earl Fraser, who designed this nickel, grew up near the Plains Indians in the Dakotas.

IT'S A FACT

In 1913, the United States Mint hired James Earl Fraser to design a nickel. Fraser wanted to honor the Plains Indians. He put an image of a Plains Indian on one side of the nickel and a buffalo on the other. But he could not find buffalo on the Great Plains for models. He had to travel to the Bronx Zoo in New York to look at buffalo.

CHAPTER 2

The Move to Reservations

Plains Indians and settlers continued to fight. The U.S. government wanted peace. The U.S. wanted the Plains tribes to move to reservations. Reservations were lands set aside for Native Americans.

The buffalo were gone. Most tribes agreed to move. The U.S. government promised to help the tribes. It would give them food and shelter.

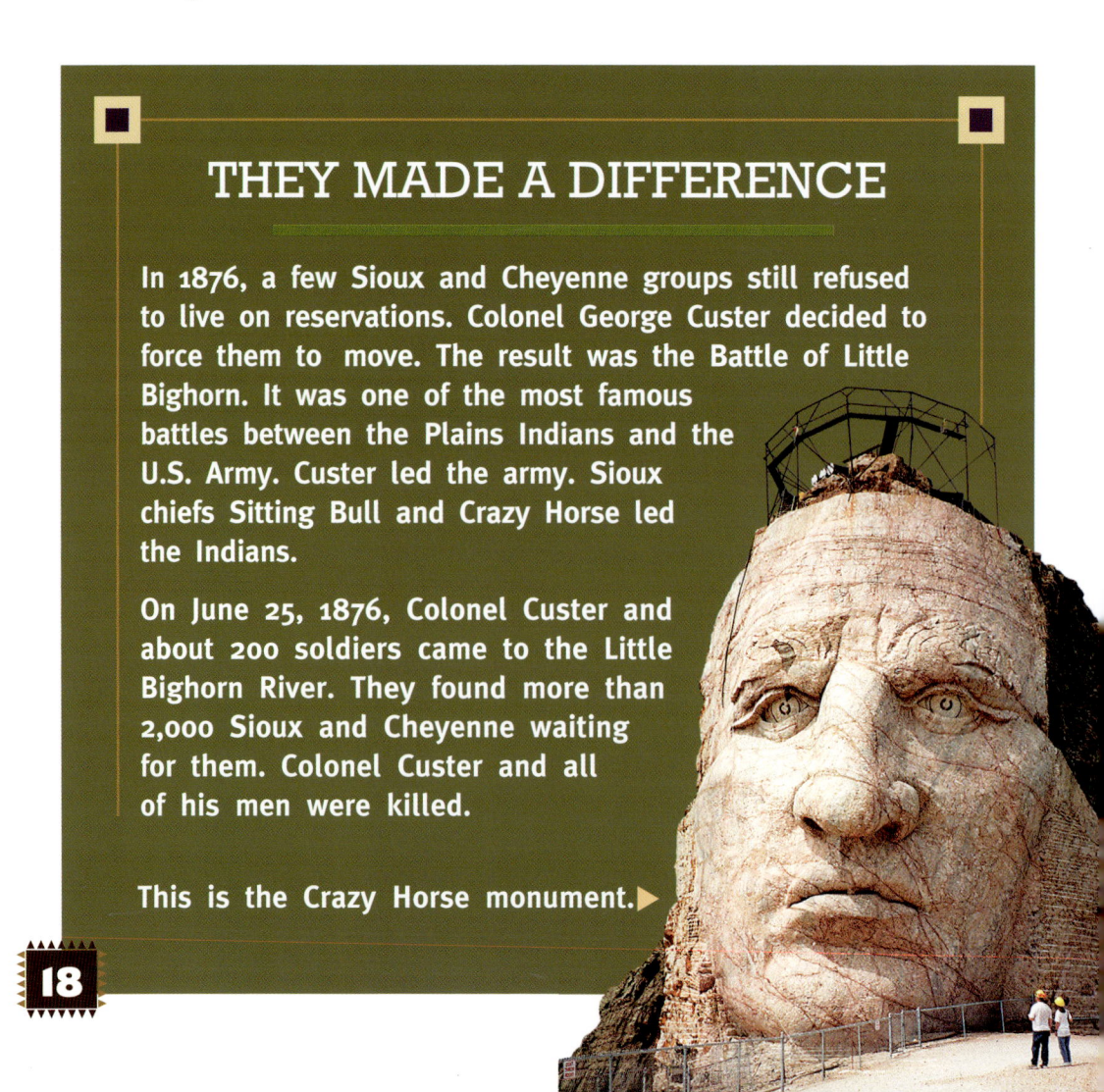

THEY MADE A DIFFERENCE

In 1876, a few Sioux and Cheyenne groups still refused to live on reservations. Colonel George Custer decided to force them to move. The result was the Battle of Little Bighorn. It was one of the most famous battles between the Plains Indians and the U.S. Army. Custer led the army. Sioux chiefs Sitting Bull and Crazy Horse led the Indians.

On June 25, 1876, Colonel Custer and about 200 soldiers came to the Little Bighorn River. They found more than 2,000 Sioux and Cheyenne waiting for them. Colonel Custer and all of his men were killed.

This is the Crazy Horse monument. ▶

CONFLICTS AND STRUGGLES

Life was different on the reservations. The Plains Indians wore cotton clothing, not leather. They lived in cloth tepees that the government gave them. Since there were very few buffalo, they did little hunting. The government gave them beef. The tribes were now poor.

Some tribes fought hard. They would not give up their land. But by 1880, all of the Plains Indians lived on reservations.

EYEWITNESS ACCOUNT

General William Tecumseh Sherman told the Plains Indians that they should not refuse to go to reservations. "You can no more stop this than you can stop the sun or moon," he warned. "You must submit and do the best you can."

CHAPTER 2

Children Go to Boarding Schools

In the late 1800s, the government started Indian schools. Thousands of Plains children left home. They went to live at boarding schools. Some of the schools were very far from home.

The children faced many changes at the schools. They had to learn English. They could not speak their own language. Boys had to cut their hair short. They had to wear clothes like the white people wore.

▲ The children gave up their traditional ways of dressing.

CONFLICTS AND STRUGGLES

▲ Jim Thorpe became a famous athlete.

IT'S A FACT

The first Indian boarding school was the Indian Industrial School in Carlisle, Pennsylvania. Lieutenant Richard Pratt established it. Lieutenant Pratt was a military officer. He believed that military habits would be good for the children. He asked them to wear uniforms. He had them march to their classrooms. They spent half of each day working with their hands. The most famous graduate of the Carlisle school was Jim Thorpe. He won two gold medals at the 1912 Olympic Games.

The U.S. made the Bureau of Indian Affairs (BIA) to run the boarding schools. The BIA wanted the Plains Indians to be like white people. They told the Plains people to give up their traditional ways. Children learn new habits more easily than adults do. So the boarding schools seemed like a good idea.

Many children missed their families and homes. Some students liked the schools. They became close with children of other tribes.

Many Native American children did not go to boarding schools. They lived at home. These children went to day schools on their reservations.

CHAPTER 3

Modern Life

In the 1930s, John Collier became the director of the Bureau of Indian Affairs. He thought Native American customs were important. He did not want the traditions to disappear. Many of the Plains Indians began to bring back their old ways. They also started new traditions.

Many Kiowa men fought in World War II. Their mothers formed women's clubs. The clubs brought back the old traditions. They danced to honor their sons' bravery. Then the men came home from the war. The men started up the old warrior society. It is called the Kiowa Gourd Clan.

▲ These men were some of the code talkers in World War II.

The Comanche revived their warrior society, too. Comanche soldiers fought in the Vietnam War. When the soldiers came home, the tribe honored them. It brought back the Little Pony Society.

Other tribes did something different. These tribes asked their best soldiers to become chiefs.

IT'S A FACT

During World War II, seventeen Comanche soldiers worked as code talkers. They helped the army send important messages in the Comanche language. The enemy was not able to understand them. Other code talkers were Navajo from the southwestern United States.

▲ This two-man team of Navajo code talkers relayed orders over the field radio using their native language.

CHAPTER 3

Powwows on the Plains

Every August, many tribes meet in South Dakota. People travel from all over. People go for the Pine Ridge **Powwow** (POW-wow). They go to see the rodeo. They go to watch the dancing. They go to sing and hear the drums. Plains people go to show their pride.

Many reservations have powwows. One tribe hosts the powwow. Then other tribes come. Powwows bring people together. They also bring together old and new traditions.

▼ These Sioux children are wearing full ceremonial dress at a powwow in Rosebud, South Dakota.

MODERN LIFE

People sing and dance in the old ways. Members of the Kiowa Gourd Clan go to powwows. They perform the Gourd Dance. This is an old dance. The Grass Dance is also an old dance. Grass dancers dress like warriors. They cover their faces with war paint.

✓ POINT

Think About It
Why do you think the author included information about modern powwows? How does this help you better understand the importance of tradition to all cultures?

The powwow is a new tradition. One of the first powwows was held by the Comanche. It happened in the 1940s.

HISTORICAL PERSPECTIVE

The Crow Fair is another large summer event. It is on the Crow tribe's reservation in Montana. The fair is similar to the Pine Ridge Powwow. The Crow Fair is much older, though. The Bureau of Indian Affairs started it in 1904. The bureau wanted a very different sort of fair. They thought the Crow should display farm animals. Over time, the Crow made a lot of changes. The fair came to look like their old summer gatherings. Today, the fair is a popular tourist event. People come from all over the world to see it.

CHAPTER 3

Plains Indian Arts and Crafts

Arts and crafts are another tradition. Plains Indians use art to connect with their past. Artists help keep a tribe's culture alive.

Many Plains Indian women made quillwork. They used porcupine quills to make bright designs. They dyed the quills with natural dyes. The dyes came mainly from plants. Then the women wove the quills into clothing. Some quillworkers keep this tradition alive today. Other craftspeople use leather or feathers.

CAREERS

Do you enjoy learning about old cultures? You may want to become a curator. A curator is in charge of museum exhibits. A curator becomes an expert on a few subjects. For example, you could become an expert on Native American crafts. You might spend some time on a reservation watching a Native American potter make bowls. Then you could organize a special pottery exhibit at your museum.

◀ Quillworkers soften the porcupine quills in their mouths. That makes them easier to work with.

MODERN LIFE

Plains painters still make traditional paintings. In the early 1900s, five Kiowa painters became famous. They were known as the "Kiowa Five." They helped create future Native American artists.

Some Plains people are also great writers. Vine Deloria, Jr. is from the Sioux tribe. N. Scott Momaday is a Kiowa. A member of the Osage (OH-saje) tribe became a great ballet dancer. Her name is Maria Tallchief. She has danced all over the world.

THEY MADE A DIFFERENCE

Ben Nighthorse Campbell is a member of the Cheyenne tribe. He served in the House of Representatives from 1987 to 1993. Then he was elected to the U.S. Senate. He served there from 1993 to 2005. Campbell encouraged the U.S. government to build the National Museum of the American Indian in Washington, D.C. Campbell is also an artist. He makes traditional Native American jewelry.

CHAPTER 3

◀ The National Museum of the American Indian in Washington, D.C. opened in 2004. It is the first national museum that focuses on Native Americans.

Conclusion

For thousands of years, Native Americans lived on the Great Plains. The buffalo gave these people almost everything they needed.

In the 1700s, the Plains tribes began to keep horses. The men became better hunters. Their families had more food and clothing.

In the 1800s, the lives of the Plains people changed. The United States was growing. Thousands of settlers traveled west. White hunters killed nearly all of the buffalo. The Plains Indians fought with settlers. Their old way of life was gone.

The U.S. government wanted peace on the Plains. The U.S. made tribes move to reservations. Life on the reservations was very hard. Still, the Plains Indians stayed proud.

CONCLUSION

Today, all Native Americans are U.S. citizens. They do not have to live on reservations. Still, many choose to. Many tribes brought back their old customs. They have also begun new traditions.

Today, many Americans celebrate the Plains Indians. People go to powwows on the Plains. In schools, students learn about Native American history.

Time Line

Early 1700s	The Plains Indians get horses from southwestern Indians.
1840s	Thousands of white pioneers ride through the Great Plains on their way west.
1848	Gold is discovered in California. Thousands of people cross the Plains Indians' hunting grounds.
1851	Eight Plains Indian tribes meet with government officials. The tribes agree to stay inside their hunting grounds.
1860s	Professional white hunters begin killing millions of buffalo.
1867	The Arapaho, Cheyenne, Comanche, and Kiowa tribes agree to live on reservations.
1876	On June 25, the Battle of Little Bighorn takes place in what is now Montana. Sioux and Cheyenne warriors kill Colonel George Custer and his men.
1880	All of the Plains Indians live on reservations.
1933	The Bureau of Indian Affairs no longer prevents the Plains Indians from enjoying their customs and traditions.
2004	The National Museum of the American Indian opens in Washington, D.C.

Glossary

adapt (uh-DAPT) to change in order to survive (page 3)

conflict (KAHN-flikt) a fight or war (page 14)

nomad (NOH-mad) a person with no permanent home who wanders in search of food or water (page 2)

plain (PLANE) a large, flat region covered in grass but with few trees (page 2)

powwow (POW-wow) a Native American ceremony (page 24)

reservation (reh-zer-VAY-shun) land set aside by the government for use by Native Americans (page 3)

tan (TAN) to make into leather by soaking in a special solution (page 17)

tepee (TEE-pee) a tent shaped like a cone, made from animal skins or cloth stretched over poles (page 4)

Index

adapt, 3
Arapaho, 11, 23, 30
arts, 26–27
boarding schools, 20–21
buffalo, 2–6, 8–10, 14, 16–19, 29–30
ceremonies, 12–13
Cheyenne, 11, 18, 27, 30
Comanche, 6–8, 15, 23, 30
conflict, 14–21
family, 4, 9–10, 21, 29
Hidatsa, 8–9
horse, 4–7, 12–13, 29–30

Kiowa, 15, 22, 25, 27, 30
nomad, 2, 5
plain, 2–3, 6, 11, 14–18, 24, 29–30
powwow, 24–25, 30
reservation, 3, 18–19, 21, 24–26, 29–30
Sioux, 10–12, 18, 24, 27, 30
Sun Dance, 12–13
tan, 17
tepee, 4–5, 10, 12, 19
villages, 2, 4–6, 8–9
warrior societies, 11, 22–23, 30